FATAL

The incredible untold stories of the most famous female spies in history

M.K GRACE

Table of Contents

C. R. Rees.

Introduction

Congratulations on purchasing this book and thank you for doing so.

The following chapters will discuss the most famous female spies and how they were able to get the most information during wartime. It will also go over *why* female spies are the best and how they have made history.

There are plenty of books on this subject on the market, thanks again for choosing this one! Every effort was made to ensure it is full of as much useful information as possible, please enjoy!

Chapter 1: Why Are Female Spies the Best?

When most people think of the common spy, they think of the dapper agent who likes his drinks a certain way and always has a beautiful woman trailing behind him but what if the best spies were actually the women who were trailing behind 007? This would be more accurate to the truth of the way that the world works because, in a surprising turn of things, women actually make some of the best spies. There are many reasons for this and women have been working as spies for as far back as the beginning of time. Since female spies *do* make the best agents, let's look at some of the reasons why.

Unexpected Career Choice

Even though female spies are often able to do better work than their male counterparts, it is still a relatively rare career choice for women. Because of this, it makes them less of a suspect when it comes to figuring out who a spy is. Most people would not even think of the woman who is in the typical "spy" story being the spy who makes it much safer for the woman to be able to spy on the different things that are going on and get the information that she needs. Females are not usually expected to be spies which make them better spies because they have far less suspicion that follows them around when they are doing things.

One of the things that *make* women better spies is actually able to be used to allow them to have a career choice in the field of spying. Even though there are many different reasons a woman could be better at being a spy than a man who was doing the same job, there are also reasons that she is able to fit in within the spy world to get the most out of the jobs that she has to do. The unexpected career choice is something that women will always need to look out for when they are trying to figure out the right way to spy on men and what is going on with each of them.

When a woman chooses a career as a spy and is actually good at what she does, there is less of a chance that she will be caught spying simply because of the fact that she is a woman. While it is now commonly accepted that women can do anything that men can do, many people still have a hard time believing that a female would be able to do the same type of spy work that a male is also able to do.

Ability to Transform

If you've ever been to a drag show, you know that it can be hard to make a man look like a realistic woman. Men who dress in drag are professionals and, most of the time, it is *still* hard to believe that they are a woman. On the contrary, the chances are that you have seen a woman who is dressed like a man and never even thought twice about it. Women are better able to disguise themselves as men than men are able to disguise themselves as women. Their ability to transform is not only better but also much easier for them to do.

As you are reading through the list, you will find that many of the most famous female spies were masters of disguise. This means that they were able to disguise themselves almost perfectly. You may also notice the common theme that many of them disguised themselves as men. They needed to do this in most instances to be able to get into the places that they wanted. There were not many times throughout history where women were able to get into the military or even into government positions that would give them access to what they needed to know. Not only did they need to get *into* these places, they often had to do so as a man.

Different Way of Thinking

While men and women are equal, it is scientific knowledge that their brains work in different ways. Women have a tendency to be able to think of different solutions and "outside of the box" in a way that men just are unable to do. They can bring in a different approach to the way of thinking. This is especially useful during times of war – which is a male-dominated industry. The female spies are able to come in and think of different ways to do things and ways to get to things so that they are able to get the information that they want. Female spies bring a different approach to the table and are able to provide more information to the people who are in the different fields.

It is important to note that having a female perspective will often work when there are groups of spies or when a spy needs to be able to get the information that she wants. She will just need to think differently from the men who should come naturally to female spies. Doing this will give them the help that they need to be able to get the answers that they want. It will also allow them the chance to be able to learn as much as they can about the information that they need to be a spy to get.

Even though not all women are going to be guaranteed to think the same way, the female mind has different approaches to things. It can be helpful in a sea of men who are all thinking the same way when new solutions need to be proposed.

Fewer Problems When Spying

If a female is spying and she is caught doing so, she may be able to get "off the hook" more easily than a man would. While it is not necessarily morally correct, many prosecutors will look at the fact that the spy was a woman. They may allow her a different type of sentence than they would a man which can make the risks far reduced for women who are spying and in the industry. This is something that many female spies never consider – to think about being caught may mean that they will be more inclined to be caught – but it is something that will help them if it *does* occur.

It is important to note that not all females get "off the hook" when they are working as spies. This is evidenced in several of the most famous female spies. While they were not given easy sentences, they were given the exact opposite. The prosecutors of these spies wanted to show the women as an example and make sure that others knew that things would not be tolerated. The way that female spies were

often punished was with death for the reason of espionage during or not during wartime.

Chapter 2: Nancy Wake: The White Mouse with an Arm

"I hate wars and violence, but if they come then, I don't see why we women should just wave our men a proud goodbye and then knit them balaclavas."
– Nancy Wake

Nancy Wake was a free spirit from the time she was a child until she worked for the French Resistance. She was always working to do more, to be more and to fight the bigger powers that had her locked in a hypothetical cage where she was forced to knit for some man. Nancy Wake worked first as a nurse and then as an eventual spy, fighting the Gestapo and, eventually, killing one with her bare hands.

CARTE D'IDENTITÉ

Nom CARLIER

Prénoms Lucienne Suzanne

Profession

Nationalité Française

Domicile

SIGNALEMENT

Taille

Cheveux

Bouche

Yeux

Visage

Teint clair

Signes particuliers

Établi à

Le 10 FEV 1942

Enregistré sous le N°

CHANGEMENTS SUCCESSIFS DE DOMICILE

Cachet Officiel

Cachet Officiel

Using Her Female Features

After The White Mouse entered into the special forces and became a spy for the French Resistance, she wanted to do different things that no other spy would have been able to do during the time that they were in the war. She used her femininity to play into the Nazi soldiers and to try to get them to where she wanted them so that she would be able to spy on them in the way that she wanted and, eventually, use her special forces training to defeat them.

When all of this was going on, she would simply slip into the areas where the guards were for the concentration camps. This was something that she could do easily. She had a bubbly personality, and she was very flirtatious. The guards had her mistaken for a floozy who just wanted to learn more about their job. They thought that she was going to be someone who just wanted to see what was going on.

In reality, Wake really did just want to see what was going on. Her motives for this, though, were much different than what the SS guards suspected that she was going to do. She was going to the camps, collecting information and using it as motivation to help get the Jewish people to safer places. While she didn't necessarily smuggle any of them out like some of the other spies, she got the information that she needed to make a difference. It was enough to make her want to fight even harder to be a spy and to get the people the help that they needed.

Infiltrating the Gestapo

Once she realized that her charming personality and her much-needed beauty during the time of war was something that would help her to get in with the Gestapo, she used all of this to her own advantage. She flirted with passion, she made sure to draw the men in, and she did a lot of different things that set her apart from other spies. All of these things gave her the ammunition that she needed to go back to the allies and to give them what they were asking for. This was something that allowed her the chance to do more.

She did this for several different times before she was found out and it gave her a great chance at collecting information that would prove to be extremely valuable when it came to the defeat of the Nazis. She wanted to collect information so that she could help the suffering Jews who she saw so often in the camps that she was spying in. If she had been able to, she would have carted each one of them out of the camp at the time, but she knew that her mission had a much bigger purpose.

Special Operations with a Bounty

Nancy Wake was a special operations executive. She was one of the most popular spies and was able to get what she needed from the different things that were going on during the time that she was in Nazi Germany and in other areas that were occupied by Hitler's army. She tried hard, but she was eventually found out by the higher ups. This did not stop her, though. She still continued to be a spy, and that was something that risked her own life. It was also the way that she was able to eventually get exactly what she needed from them.

Since many of the people who were lower down on the totem pole did not know who she was, she was able to (for a short time) continue to spy on them. It became too dangerous when the SS army put a price of 5 million francs on her head. She fled the country but she continued to fight for the allies, and she was always trying to get to the front of the action where she thought that she would be able to get the most out of the war that was going on.

Bare Handed Killing

During her time in the special operations training, she learned some moves that were like hand to hand combat and the moves showed her what she would be able to do if she just set her mind to it. She did not think that she would ever need to participate in hand to hand combat because she always had a weapon, but she remembered the training if she needed it. It was a good thing that she was able to remember it because she ended up needing it not long after she had learned how to fight hand to hand.

She was confronted with an SS soldier face to face. This was something that she had never expected but something that still happened when she was in the city. She knew that she had training and her judo chopped him to the throat as soon as she realized who he was. She did not think that the judo chop would work, but she knew that she had to do something. The White Mouse was surprised when the soldier dropped dead on the ground.

The White Mouse had killed an enemy soldier with her own bare hands … or, rather, bare forearm.

Loss of the War Time

Even though Nancy Wake saw a lot of success in her own military career, her husband was not quite as lucky as she was. He did not leave France when she did. He had been captured, tortured and killed. This was because the Army was looking for her and, once they learned that he was her husband, they did what they could to get back at her. It was something that was extremely demeaning and caused her to question whether anything that she did was really worth it.

Despite the fact that she had lost her husband during the war, Nancy Wake did not let this crush her spirit. She still always fought for what was right although she made a choice to not participate in any more spy missions or judo chops. She became influential in the British army, though, and was able to help people get the information that they needed when it came to spying. She even had an entire course that was dedicated to female spies where she taught women that they could be spies and that they could actually use the fact that they were females to help them become better at spying.

Fatal

Chapter 3: Mata Hari: The Spy of Dancing Mystery

"I have never done an act of espionage against France. Never. Never."

-- *Mata Hari*

Mata Hari has a lot of mystery surrounding her life, her death, and espionage. She was someone who, essentially, fabricated a life for herself out of nothing. There is no clear record of where she was officially from or where she was brought up. The fact that she was most commonly known by her stage name made it difficult to find much information about her when people were putting together information about her life, but there are a few things that are certain.

A Woman of Passion

Hari was someone who believed in passion, love and living her life in a way that exemplified her love of life. It was something that she knew how to do well, and something that she wanted to make sure would always work for her. She never thought that living her life as a dancer was something that she was going to turn into a career that would eventually lead to her dying because of her actions.

As a dancer, she took a lot of risks. Even though France was famous for exotic dances and dancers who truly tried to "bear it all" Mata Hari was not *that* type of woman. She did do a lot of dances, and most of them involved her shedding layers upon layers of scarves as she danced, but she did it in a way that was filled with tact and class. She always kept a brassiere on but was not afraid to show off her bottom. She even rode horses nearly naked, and that allowed her to be set apart from the different dancers of the time.

Beauty in the Dance

She did not want to dance just to please men or to make money. She did it because she was comfortable with it and she saw it as a type of art. She knew that there was a lot of beauty in the dances that she did, and she always tried to show off the skills that she had. She touted herself as a Hindu dancer and someone who was able to shroud a lot of different secrets under the scarves that she kept herself covered with. It was a way for her to be able to get the most out of the different things that she had. She wanted people to be able to enjoy her dances aside from the fact of pleasing men in a sensual way.

The dances that she did were, in fact, beautiful. They were designed around the Indian culture, and they had a lot of different moves to them. It took a lot of skill on her part, and she had to make sure that she was doing the best job possible when it came to her dances. She did not want to give up the illusion that she was truly a Hindu dancer and that she had learned all of her skills in that way.

Country Hopping

One that was definitely sure about Mata Hari was that she was from the country of Holland. Anyone knew her deeper than from just one of her dances was able to see that she was from Holland. Despite her exotic looks, her vast knowledge of the dances and her scarves that kept all of her secrets, she was not that exotic, and she was certainly not from Egypt, India or any of the places that she may have claimed to be from.

Since she was from Holland, she was able to move about freely in Europe even though there was a World War going on. This was because Holland was neutral and she was confident in the way that she was able to do things. She was not worried about being caught because she really wasn't doing anything wrong. She was just traveling from country to country with her trunk full of scarves and the ability that she had to make people happy. It was something that she felt she needed to do each time that she went to a new country.

Later on in Her Life

Mata Hari eventually was too old to dance. She was getting larger, older and nobody really had much of interest in her. She still performed for the soldiers and even some of the higher ups in the military, but it was more for fun than it was for any type of truly pleasurable entertainment. She needed to make sure that she was able to make money and this was the only way to do it. She also offered special favors to the people who she danced for in exchange for some extra money for the dances that she performed. Her career in dancing and making men happy became all about money, and she tried her hardest to get money.

After being with a Russian soldier who was almost 20 years her junior, she found that she needed to make even more money. He was hurt when he was hit by a bullet, and she became the sole provider for their family. She took on jobs like she had never done before and these jobs often involved doing favors for the military. The French military actually asked her to use her powers over other militaries and her ability to jump from country to country to spy on German soldiers. She did just that.

Double Crossing Agent

What the French military never predicted is that they would intercept correspondence that named Mata Hari as a spy for the German people. The Germans did this because they knew that she was a spy for the French. They knew what she was trying to do and it was something that they did not like, so they put her up as a double crosser and tried to have her taken away on their terms. The French chose to execute her because of the espionage.

Despite the fact that she was executed, it could never be completely proven that she had double-crossed them. This was something that remains speculation to this day and something that will probably never be known. While Mata maintained her innocence until the day that she was executed by firing squad, there is a large chance that she *was* a spy for Germany. This could have explained the country hopping of her earlier days and the affinity that she had for soldiers. There was a good chance that she was a spy and that is what she was doing the entire time that she was performing as a dancer.

Because she had somewhat of a seedy past and there was nothing official about her except her country of origin (one that was, in fact, close to Germany), it was hard for her to prove that she was not a spy. There was a high chance that she had been a spy throughout her entire career and that, not her dancing, is what led to her demise, and she eventually downfalls when she was executed for espionage by the French army for being a double agent against France.

Chapter 4: Noor Inayat Khan: Pacifist Turned Spy

"Liberty!"

-- Noor Inayat Khan's last word, after being beaten, tortured and raped for hours

Unlike many of the spies in this series that have happy endings or endings where they are caught for double crossing, Noor Inayat Khan is one of the only ones who has a noble, while still devastating, a death that stands behind her. At only 30 years old, she was killed in a concentration camp for being a spy against the German army. She also had some problems with the army that led to that point, but she always let them know that she was, in fact, a fighter against their beliefs and the things that they did.

Starting Out

Noor was one of the people who would have been the least likely to be chosen to be a spy. She had an Indian father and an American mother. She was raised in France and, before being a spy, she wrote a lot of children's stories, studied music and was planning a career to become a teacher for children who needed someone to help them with the arts. This was something that she was able to do very well, but things changed when the war came to Paris.

Noor and her brother both thought that it would be a good idea to work together with the allies. Since they were Indian and American, they thought that they could set an example for the rest of the people when there was a lot of tension in the way that things worked. They also wanted to make a difference for the country that they loved and held dear to their hearts because it was something that they were passionate about.

After joining the movement, Noor found that she was very skilled at wireless communication. This put her up for a spot with the French special operations division and gave her a chance to make a name for herself in the war while also helping out. She was one of the best and was actually one of the only wireless communicators who was left in France at the time that Paris was occupied by Nazis. It was a way for her to continue helping her country even though she knew that she was putting herself at risk for the things that she did.

For France

IDENTITY CARD FOR R.A.F. AND W.A.A.F. PERSONNEL (All Ranks)

Women's Auxiliary Air Force

754197

All of the help that she did was for France. It was her way of showing her commitment to the country and her way of doing different things with the country. As a wireless operator, she was able to spy on conversations and learn more about what was going on with Germany. She was even taken out of Paris at the direction of the special operations, but she continued to go back despite the fact that her bosses thought that she was too fragile to handle the communication aspect of different things that were going on. She knew that she was not too fragile and that she was going to be able to do more for Paris than anyone who had come before she was able to do.

It was during this time that she was captured and she had to be tortured as a spy. This was what the German army did to people who were spies during this time. It was something that she knew would happen. She also knew that her death was imminent and that she was going to have to pay for spying even though it was the noble thing to do. She wanted to make sure that she was able to get the most out of working with the allies and did not care that she was going to have to deal with the problems that came along with being caught for espionage.

A Small Mistake

The mistake that did her in was the fact that she continued to operate on the wireless long after there were no other people. Having a single target to go after made it easier for the Germans to find her and to take her as a prisoner for being a spy. It was something that was not expected but something that still had her taken into the custody of Germany so that they could eventually kill her.

What the Germans found was so much more than what they had bargained for. She had been taking notes as a spy when she was operating wirelessly. She would not talk when she was captured, but the Germans found that they did not need her to talk. She had been keeping track of everything that was going on during the time that she was talking on the wireless in a notebook. All they had to do was use it, and they could actually continue talking as if they were here. This is what caused her greatest shame.

Used Against Allies

Since the Germans were able to continue pretending like they were Noor even after she was captured, there were allies who were killed as a result. They used her abilities to be able to capture them. While it did not take long for the allies to catch on, it did result in the death of three ally soldiers who were coming to her rescue when she had already been captured and when she was already on her way to be killed.

While Noor knew what was going on and knew that she had made a mistake, she was still shamed into thinking that things were her fault. She knew that she should not have kept a notebook, but it was something that she was able to keep track with. Even though it was a small mistake that wouldn't have ordinarily made a difference in the way that things were done, it was a problem for Noor and caused her to become shameful about what she did. It didn't matter, though, because she was already slated to be killed in a concentration camp with other female spies who were also captured.

The Fight Continued

Despite the fact that Noor was captured, tortured, raped and beaten, she still continued to be a fighter. This was much different from what she had learned as a pacifist, but she was also taught that she should fight for everything that she believed in and liberty was one of the biggest things that she did believe in. She continued to fight. She was labeled as a dangerous person in the prison that she was in and that was something that she knew that she was going to have to contend with when she wanted to get the most out of the situation that she was in.

It is important to note that she continued to fight even after she was sent to the concentration camp. The people who arrived there with her will killed as soon as they got there. The officers had specific instructions, though, to do everything that they could to make her death as painful and drawn out as possible. Even though she had been raped, beaten and tortured for hours (or maybe even days) before she was killed, she still continued to fight. She was weak and dying before she was shot, but sources reported that she built up enough strength to scream out the word "Liberty!" one last time before she was shot.

Fatal

Noor Inayat Khan always fought for liberty and for the freedom of people from the way that the Germans had taken over. Her death was one that was filled with nobility and there was no shame in the mistake that she had made with the notebook.

Chapter 5: Virginia Hall: Danger with a Limp

"I am living pleasantly and wasting time. It isn't worthwhile, and after all, my neck is my own. If I am willing to get a crick in it, I think that's my prerogative." – Virginia Hall

Touted as the most dangerous spy in the Allies by the German people during the second World War. She was an American who came from a very wealthy upbringing. After being close to a lot of military action in Baltimore, Maryland where there was a lot of different things going on, she recognized that it would be her calling to serve in the military. What she did not realize, though, is that her talents were better suited to working as an operator on the radio and being one of the most dangerous (according to Hitler's army) and influential (according to the Allies) spies of the entire World War.

Virginia Hall was able to effectively learn much more about the German army than any of the other spies which made her a major wanted woman for the Germans.

Starting Out

When Virginia was first getting started, she was sent to Spain. This is the time that she was able to get the practice that she needed when she was listening in on the various conversations that went on with the German army. The problem, though, was that there was not much going on in Spain at the time. The Allies did not want her to go anywhere that was dangerous because they knew that she could be harmed, especially considering she had a disability.

They kept her in Spain, but she wanted to do more. She joined so that she would be able to work, help and make a difference. She recognized that she was not able to do any of this in Spain. She fought for her right to be able to work in Nazi-occupied Paris, and she won the ability to go there and use the radio.

Suitcase Radios

The radio that she worked off of was so small that she carried it around in a suitcase. This also helped to make her look less conspicuous and less of a target when it came to figuring out if she was a spy. To the Nazis, she was just a woman walking down the street with her bag, albeit she did somewhat stick out because of the limp that she had. The suitcase radio helped her to be less obvious to the Germans who were looking for the "most dangerous spy" with a big radio.

The suitcase radio that she used was able to help her learn where drop zones were, find POWs and help to rescue people from the Germans who had taken them captive. She hid out in rooms in different areas around the city, and she snuck around getting to where she wanted to be. It was a dangerous job but one that she enjoyed doing because she knew that she was making a difference and helping to save the lives of many people who were a part of the special operations.

Cuthbert Was Always by Her Side

Unlike many of the female spies who are considered the best of all time, Virginia Hall had an unwavering companion who was with her for every interaction that she had.

Cuthbert.

This is the name that she gave to her artificial leg. She had been injured in a hunting accident when she was just a young woman and had lost her leg as a result. She was outfitted with an artificial leg, but she still had a limp from the way that her leg worked and from the different things that were going on with it. She had some trouble with it at times, especially when she was escaping Paris. One of the messages that she received actually told her to eliminate Cuthbert if she had to...people who knew Hall knew that she called the leg Cuthbert.

This is just one example of the type of woman that she was. She was witty, she had a great sense of humor, and she did things like name her leg Cuthbert. She was not only the most dangerous spy that the Nazis ever had but she was also someone who had a lot of different layers to herself – she was truly a woman with a bold personality. The Germans, though, did not know about Cuthbert. It was one part of Virginia that they did not know even though many suspected it because of the limp that she had.

The Search Continues

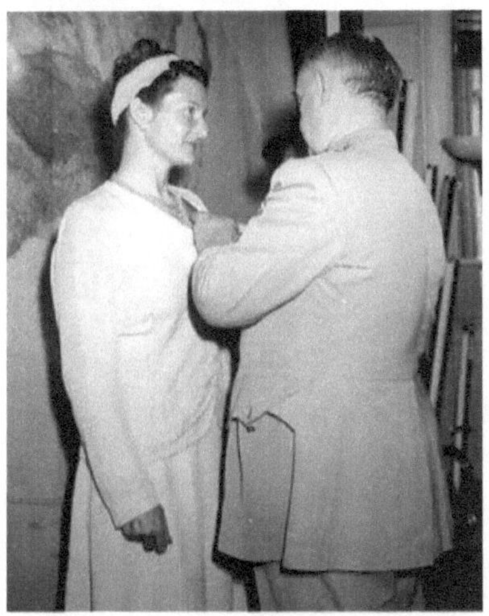

Throughout the time that Virginia Hall was serving in Nazi Paris, she was always making waves. She took a lot of risks that almost always panned out for her and she was able to get the help that she needed when she saved people from the Nazis. She was a spy who not only knew what she was doing but who was also unafraid to take the risks that were required for her to be able to do good at her job.

The Nazis always wanted to find her. They thought that finding her would be the key to winning the war. She kept giving their secrets away and was regarded as someone who was dangerous. While they knew that she was a woman who limped, there was not much else that they knew about her. They also wanted to make sure that they were able to find her so they did everything that they could. This led to her being one of the most sought after spies of the World War, and it caused them to get frustrated with the different things that were going on during that time.

Recognition for Services

Since Virginia Hall was such a great spy and she was able to save so many people all while doing it on one "real" leg and without ever being found out by the German army, she got a great deal of recognition for her services. She remained humble, though, and until her death, she continued to say that it was only six years of her life and she should not be thought of as only that service. She did not want to "cash in" on her experiences as many other spies from that time had done previously.

When she was the only civilian to receive a medal, she requested that it not be done with a large fanfare. She wanted only her mother and the general who was giving it to her to be present. She believed that she was deserving of it, but she also believed that many other people were deserving of the ceremonial rights that came along with it. She did not want to overshadow them and certainly did not want to make a big deal about something that she felt was her own duty to do.

Chapter 6: Ethel Rosenberg: The Great Bad Spy

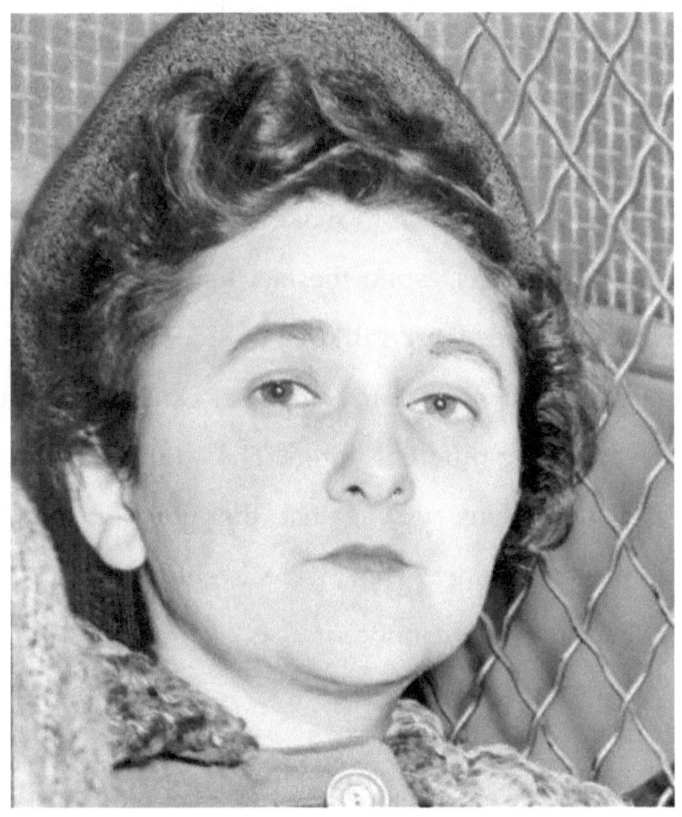

"I refuse to answer on the ground that this might be incriminating."

– Ethel Rosenberg

Fatal

Ethel Rosenberg was a spy companion with her husband. They worked for the Soviet Union during the time of the Cold War, and that was what incriminated them as spies. Despite the fact that they did not want to be found out, there were many things that they did that set them up for failure from the beginning of their career as spies and it was something that eventually led to them losing the hold that they had in the community that they were in and it was something that allowed them the chance to make sure that they were able to declare their innocence. Despite the fact that they maintained that they were innocent, they were still tried and, ultimately, executed for the information that they gave to the Soviet Union during that time when they were doing different things. They did not stand a chance when it came to going up against the government they had committed treason against. They were eventually found out, but some still believe they were innocent.

As a Couple

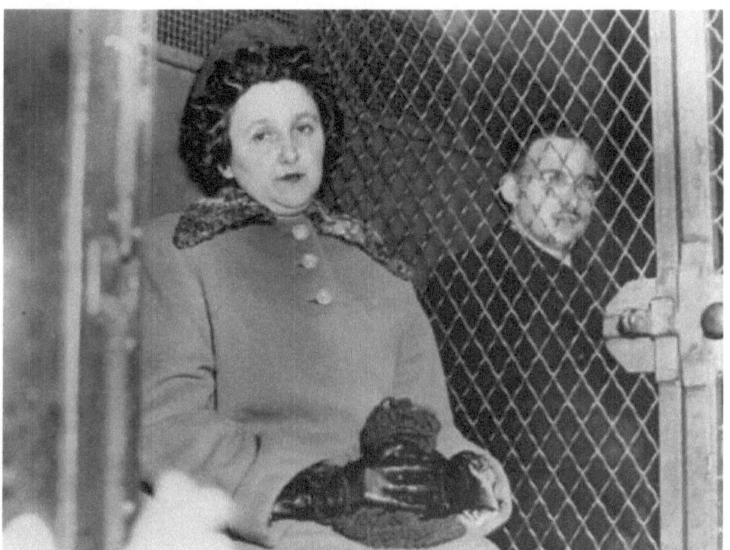

When Ethel started out her spy career, she worked exclusively with her husband, Julius. This was because he was the one who was originally a spy and he got her involved with his espionage. He wanted her to do the things that he did because he thought that having a feminine side to things would be able to help him from getting caught with the spy activity that he was doing. It was something that he chose to bring his wife into and risk her getting in as much trouble as him.

The thing is, though, Ethel probably would have been tried either way. She maintained that she was innocent and she was still tried and executed for the things that Julius did. While there were some ways in which the government could prove that she was a spy, she did try to only do what Julius told her to in the beginning. Like most of the spies who are in this book (even though Ethel is not someone on the side of the "good" guys), she had her own opinions and was fiercely independent even when it came to the things that her husband wanted her to do.

Ethel Branches Off

Even though they started out together, Ethel eventually went rogue from her husband. This was something that he did not know about and something that she wanted to keep to herself so that she would be able to get the most out of the different things that were going on in her world. She thought that she would be more successful without him and that allowed her the chance to make sure that she was doing things the right way.

When Ethel branched off, she became one of the greatest spies of her time. She learned a lot about the United States and the different things that were going to happen during the cold war. She then warned the Soviet Union about each of these things, and she wanted them to be able to stand a chance against the United States. Doing this made her guilty of espionage and caused her to be labeled as someone who was going to the different things that were going on. It was dangerous, but she felt that it was her duty to do it.

Just Answer

When Ethel was eventually found out, she was given a chance to give answers to questions that were asked about the different things that went on and the part that she played in what her husband was doing. At that point, the government had no idea that she had gone out on her own in addition to the way that she was doing things with her husband. It was something that they only found out about after they began to dig deeper into the information that they had and it was something that they had to talk with the people who were involved with.

If Ethel had just answered the questions that were asked about her husband, the government would still have no idea about the things that she was doing. She would not be *as* guilty as what she was, and the chance that she would have been executed would have been far reduced. She could have just gotten off with a slap on the wrist for not reporting what her husband did, but she chose to keep quiet and protect him which eventually led to her (and his) demise in the form of an electric chair.

He Influenced Her

The influence that Julius had over Ethel was great. He chose the things that she did, the missions that she took on and the information that she included in each of the things that she found out about the different things that were going on in the United States. It was something that made a big difference in the way that things were handled and it caused her to struggle when it came time to go against him. Despite the fact that he influenced her, she did not know what life would be like without him in it. It was something that she only had to deal with for a short period of time because she was executed not long after he was.

There were probably many things that Ethel could have done that were not involved with Julius. Just because he was her husband did not mean that she needed to follow in his footsteps. It also did not mean that she needed to do each thing that he said. He wanted to make sure that she was able to get the most out of what he was doing, so he made her follow in his own footsteps…the right to the grave.

If Only…

Many of the women included in this book are both noble and generally good human beings. It is something that the people who are included need to take into account. Ethel Rosenberg, though, was not a good person. She did what she thought was right by following her husband, ignoring her moral code and impeding her ability to live a normal life. While she was a spy like the rest of the women included, that was the only thing that she was. At least with some of the other ones who weren't necessarily on the "good" side, they were doing it for money or some other motive. Ethel was only doing it to follow in her husband's footsteps.

Despite the fact that she was a bad spy, she was one of the greatest of all time. It took the government a long time to find out about what she was doing, and that is the true mark of a great spy. It was something that she needed to make sure that she was doing right and it was a great way for her to make sure that she was getting the most out of the different things that she could do. It was also a way for her to be recognized as one of the great bad spies of all time.

Chapter 7: Mary Bowser: From Slave to Spy

"...remember everything that I saw on the desk."

– Mary Bowser

Not only did Mary Bowser have a naturally brilliant mind and a photographic memory that allowed her to remember each little detail of everything that she saw throughout her life, but she was also able to read and write. Unlike most slaves, Mary Bowser had a chance to learn thanks to her mistress. It proved to be instrumental during her time growing up and, again, when she was working for the Union during the Civil War. If it weren't for Mary Bowser's skills of being able to remember things, the Civil War might have turned out much differently from what it did.

Born a Slave

Like most African Americans who were alive during the Civil War and for a long time before it, Bowser was born into slavery. Unlike many of the other slaves who were in the country, she was born into an affluent Southern family that *cared* about their slaves.

The family did not use them for extremely grueling work and, instead, treated them much more like servants than slaves. They wanted them to be the best slaves possible, and they knew that the right way to do it was to treat them with the respect that they deserved. It was something that made quite a difference in Bowser's upbringing and gave her a chance to be able to overcome all of the difficulties that were normally aimed at slaves and the things that they did. It was something that allowed her to eventually become the most influential spy during her time.

Educated the Right Way

Since Bowser's owners knew that they had to treat their slaves in the right way, they did everything that they could to educate them and teach them about the different things that were going on in the world. They were among the only families that allowed their slaves to read and write. They actually encouraged this and even paid extra money to have them educated the right way in the North so that they would be able to read and write.

Mary Bowser was sent to the North and was educated. She learned how to read and write. She also learned a lot of different things about life and the way that it worked in the North. She knew that she wanted something more and the Van Lew family gave it to her. Since it was still illegal, technically, for them to set her free, they sent her back to live in Liberia. It actually ended up being much worse than the slave life, and she came back to Richmond to live with the Van Lews again, promising to help them out in anyway that she could. This was the point when she started her career as a spy.

Abolitionist Outlook

The thing about the Van Lew family is that they are suspected to have been an abolitionist family long before it came out that the children were abolitionists. They helped people like Harriet Tubman, and they worked to help free as many slaves as possible. They got a lot of people to freedom through the money that they had along with the connections that they had in their lives. This was something that gave them the advantage over the other people who were present in the slave trade and who were not able to get what they wanted.

While it was never officially recognized, the father of the Van Lew family was probably an abolitionist. The way that he treated his slaves shows that he was caring and compassionate – things that were both characteristics of the abolitionists in his time. His children certainly were, and they worked to help create the underground railroad. They were one of the biggest supporters of it, and they were able to make sure that many slaves got the freedom that they deserved by allowing them to pass through areas in the South to get to the North and freedom.

Coming Back to America

Once Mary Bowser came back to the United States, she wanted to make a difference for other people. She saw the way that people were treated in Liberia and that was something that she never wanted to have to witness again. She also had slave friends that needed her help, and she did everything that she could to make sure that they were able to get as free as possible. It was something that she saw as somewhat of her personal mission. She made sure each time that she did something that she was going to be able to get the help that she needed and that *she* could provide the help.

Coming back to America was one of the best things that Mary Bowser could have done for both herself and the United States. She was able to help them with the things that they needed. Despite the fact that she could read, write and was very smart, the way that she helped was somewhat unexpected. It created a turning point in the war and allowed the North to begin to win with the abolitionists eventually getting exactly what they wanted out of the war and the things that were going to happen with the war.

She was not only instrumental in helping to free slaves but also in helping the Union to win the Civil War.

In the White House

While she was in Richmond, she was offered the chance to work in The White House. This was at a time when the president was still wholly supportive of slavery and worked to make sure that people were still able to be owned by the rich families around the South. It was a part of the war when things were going to be dependent on what the president did, and the abolitionists needed to know what was going on. This is where Mary Bowser came in.

While she was working in The White House, she was able to get information. The White House recognized that she was an upper-class slave. They knew that she had not been made to do a lot of dirty work during her time in slavery and this was something that was much different from what was going on in the other areas of the South. Mary Bowser was educated, but The White House didn't know to what extent. In fact, they didn't even know that she could read or write so they allowed her into places where the president was and where important information would have been kept and written down.

Playing Dumb

Since Mary Bowser knew that the president and the people who were in charge of her did not know her secret, she decided to keep it that way. She wanted to make sure that she was always able to stay quiet about the fact that she could not only read and write well but that she also had a photographic memory. She could recall everything that she saw on the president's desk in great detail many days after she had seen it.

She used this information and continued to "play dumb" while she was working in the White House so that she would be able to make sure that she was getting the most out of it. She reported this information back to the abolitionists, and this helped the North to win the Civil War and the slaves to be freed from the shackles that had held them in place for so long. She successfully helped to end the war and to give the slaves their freedom back to the way that it used to be.

Chapter 8: Manuela Sáenz: The Mistress with a Cause

"For Bolivar, for life!"

-- Manuela Sáenz

Manuela Sáenz, like many of the other women who have been the best spies in the time that they were present, was able to use her abilities as a woman to be able to get the things that she wanted and she needed as a spy. It was something that she knew that she would be able to do when she was dating someone who was able to help her, and it was something that she also knew would come in handy when she was fighting different things. She wanted to be able to help gain freedom from Spain, and she used the fact that she was a woman to be able to do it and to get the most for her country.

Politics with Husband

When Manuela Sáenz first began working as a spy, she was very young and married to an English merchant. She had come from a different kind of background than him, and she worked hard to be able to keep up with him. One of the benefits of their relationship was that she was able to be the beauty of the operations while also learning how to be the brain.

If it weren't for having the merchant spy husband that she did who was able to help her out with different things and learning about different options in the spy world, she would not have been as successful as what she was. She also would not have met someone who was able to help make her an even better spy and been able to create freedom for many countries in South America. It was something that allowed her the chance to get what she wanted out of life and out of what it had to offer her in the form of spying on people.

There were many different things that went on in her life, but she always remembered the original politics that she had learned with her husband. She kept that in mind when she was doing everything with the different options and when she was trying to do new spy things. It allowed her the chance to make sure that she was getting the most out of the process and that she was going to be able to get more from the chance at spying for a cause.

As a Mistress to Bolivar

The time came when she had to depart her husband. It was better for her spy career if she was able to work alone and she was able to do that with the help of Bolivar. She was his mistress, and he claimed that she was the one who was able to liberate him even though he was the liberator of the country that he was in. She allowed him the chance to learn more about war, fighting for freedom and everything in between when she was with her husband.

She used her knowledge she had learned with her original husband to be a successful mistress with Bolivar. It gave her a chance to learn more about the different things and to also teach him about the different things that were going on during that time. When she was working with Bolivar, she taught him about the politics of separating from a country, and he taught her how to be a more successful spy. She knew what she was doing, and they were both able to help each other. They also were very passionate about each other and were able to grow a relationship despite tensions in the outside world.

Escape from Bogota

Since Manuela Sáenz was so good at what she did, she was able to help Bolivar escape from Bogota. This was something that she knew she would be able to do but he questioned her abilities on. He had to get out of there – there was no other option – but he also knew that it could be very risky. She took this into account, and she did her best to be able to try different things and to get him out of the country. It allowed her the chance to do more with her life and to help increase the things that were going to happen in the future.

When Manuela Sáenz helped Bolivar escape, she knew that things were meant to be. They were able to live a happy life until his death when things started to get bad again in the countries that were a part of Central America. It was something that allowed her the chance to, again, go back to her spy ways and be able to get different things from what she was doing in each of the spy fields that she was a part of.

Helping Out South America

Not only did Manuela Sáenz work with people who were her lovers but she also worked for the good of the continent as a whole. She wanted to be able to help people know that they were going to be safe in the countries that they were in. She helped with many South American countries and allowed them to be able to be free. Her spy skills were very useful when a country was trying to fight to get their independence from a different country, and it allowed her the chance to make sure that she was getting the most out of the different atmospheres.

There were many different things that happened during the time that she was a spy and she really began to make a name for herself. She knew that things were going to get better and people were constantly trying to get what they could out of her. They needed her spy skills to be able to learn more about the enemy and to be able to sneak people out of the countries so that they would be as safe as possible. It also allowed her the chance to make sure that she was getting the most out of the things that were going on along with the money that came with it.

Death in Poverty

None of this made a difference in the end, though. She eventually lost the fame that she had gained and this was something that was detrimental to her. She died poor and alone after living the last 25 years of her life in poverty. Nobody knew that she was a great spy, nobody cared, and she did not get any more help after the countries had gained their freedom. She essentially became useless because there was no cause for her to go with or go up against.

There was a chance that things would have been different if she had been anything more than a mistress to Bolivar. Since they were not official, she could not reap the benefits that came along with being his wife. She would have had a great inheritance when he died if that were the case. That would have allowed her to live off of it in the time leading up to her death, but she did not have it, so she was poor, lonely and broken down into a much worse off woman at the end of her life.

Chapter 9: Agent 355: Unknown to Most

Most of the women who are on this list we know the names of. They have made a name for themselves or others have ousted them as the spies. One of the hallmarks of a great spy, though, is never revealing your true identity. Agent 355 did exactly that. 355 was one of the most dangerous spies in the American Revolution. The only thing that is known for sure about this agent is that she was a spy and she was a woman. There is nothing else that has been officially confirmed and even nearly 300 years later, people are still trying to figure out who Agent 355 was.

Aside from the fact that she was a woman and she worked as a United States spy during the Revolution, everything else that is known about Agent 355 is just speculation.

Culper Ring

There was a ring of spies who were prominent during the time of the American Revolution. These spies all had different identities within the ring. Like most of the other spies who are included in this book, they had spy names that could identify themselves to each other and separate from one another but would not allow the enemy to be able to identify them. While some of them choose regular names that were just pseudonyms, the majority of them choose names that were just numbered. Things like "Agent 355" were not uncommon in that ring.

Despite the fact that America wasn't really all that big during that period of time, the ring of spies was relatively big and made up of people who had all different professions and came from different walks of life. Some of them were simply people who wanted to help out. Others were people who had a political interest in the United States, and others came from prominent families who wanted to help out to keep their name good. Furthermore, there were even people who were soldiers who were members of this ring.

They all worked together and learned as much about what the British were planning on doing. They also met up with other people who were working in combination with them and on their own to get the most help possible. This was one of the first rings of spies in America, but it was also one of the biggest. Some even say that this is what eventually turned into the idea for the CIA.

Family Possibilities

One thing that people noted was that the numbers often stood for codes. They could have been codes for letters, a secret way of talking or something similar. They wanted to be able to talk freely, so they used numbers to do so instead of letters. The numbers that were in the Agent 355 code could have just been random, but they also could have been code for something that meant a prominent family name in the colonies.

The chances of the woman being a prominent figure are high because she would have had even more of a reason to keep her identity secure. They would have already been targets for the British because they were rich but being a spy would have guaranteed that she would be a target and would have to deal with the consequences of committing espionage. It is a good idea to recognize that she would have been killed immediately if she were a spy. There wouldn't have even been a trial for her if she were found out so she needed to work hard to keep her identity hidden.

Husband's Imprisonment

One of the only things that *are* known about Agent 355 is that either she or her husband was imprisoned on a prison ship that was kept in the harbor. This was something that was known because she would have been able to either take him food to the prison or she would have been there herself. She would have also had a husband because there is a record that Agent 355 was pregnant at one point and that she had to deal with having a baby in the midst of both a war and of being a spy during that war.

The chances of her husband being in prison are much greater than her being in prison. It would have been nearly impossible for her to have male visitors if she were in prison – even if it were her husband. It would have also been almost impossible for her to get pregnant while she was in that prison. The authorities also said that women would not be kept on a prison ship during that time and that there would have been a separate place for her to go to that wouldn't have been with men on the ship.

Hanging of Andre

During the time that Agent 355 was a spy, Andre was hung. He was done so for the fact that he was a traitor. He was a spy, and they had been using him. He double crossed the United States and was hung as a spy. Previously, many people had thought that she was the wife of Andre, but this was not the case. There were many things that happened when Andre died, but Agent 355 did not stop doing spy work during that time.

The hanging of Andre proved to be instrumental for the Culper Ring because it allowed them to expand on the different things that they had been planning on doing in the time that they had been working as spies. It gave them the chance to bring each of these things to the forefront and to show that they were much different than what others had previously thought about them in the time that they were working as spies. Agent 355 and the rest of the Culper Ring continued to work as spies and helped the United States to win the war and gain their freedom from Britain during that time.

Anna Strong

Many people thought that Anna Strong was Agent 355. She fit the bill nearly perfectly. She had a husband who was imprisoned on a ship, she gave birth to a baby while he was in prison and she had connections on the outside of the Culper Ring that could have translated to her being a member of it. This was something that people speculated at that time and continue to do to this day.

Anna Strong was also someone who had come from a prominent family during that time. Her family had a lot of money – they were among the richest of the time – and they had a lot of political influence. They were also very strongly opposed to the British rule and had been vocal about it during that time. While not many of them had fought directly against the British, they had been able to do different things that would allow them the chance to get more of an outlook on life and the way that things were done. It is important to note that it was never proven that Anna Strong was Agent 355, but there were also a lot of other things about the agent that nobody could really prove.

No Agent

One thing that many historians hold onto is that there was no agent 355. They thought that the code was simply something that was used to describe a female instead of something that was used to describe a specific female agent. This led them to question the way that code names were created and other information was analyzed during that time so that they would have been able to make sure that they were getting what they needed from the different parts of life and the right way to do it all.

There were also a lot of misgivings about the Culper Ring during that time. The ring was designed in a way that did not allow the information of the people who were in it to be revealed. They had kept their secrets for a long time, and they were so tightly sealed that there was not much that they would have been able to do to find them. It has been a long time since the Culper Ring was a part of the way that the United States worked and many people still do not know every person who was in it.

For that reason, Agent 355 will likely always be a mystery, but it is known that she helped to free the United States from the British rule.

Conclusion

Thank for making it through to the end of this book, let's hope it was informative and able to tell you about the different spies who were among the most influential of their time. It was created so that you would be able to get the most amount of knowledge and that you would be able to use it to your advantage.

The spies that were featured in this book risked their lives for something that they believed in. Whether it was something good or something bad, it can be concluded that they were noble in the way that they supported a cause that was close to them and able to make their lives better.

Finally, if you found this book useful in any way, a review on Amazon is always appreciated!

www.ingramcontent.com/pod-product-compliance
Lightning Source LLC
Chambersburg PA
CBHW030521290526
45786CB00004B/1566

* 9 7 8 1 5 4 4 0 3 9 0 2 2 *